THE PAPER SHOES

by Nat Gabriel

illustrated by Bob Shein

Pearson Learning Group

Bear had beautiful new shoes. They were made of red paper. Two beautiful red paper shoes!

One morning Bear was walking home. He was going home to his family.

Along the way Bear gathered flowers for his family. The wind was quite calm. The sun was hot. Bear was calm and hot too.

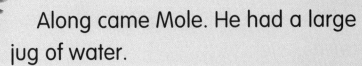

Along came Mole. He had a large jug of water.

"May I have some water?" asked Bear. "I am as hot as an oven."

"No," Mole told him. "I don't have much water."

Mole just gathered up his things and went on. Bear did not feel calm. Bear did not feel calm at all!

Bear ran ahead. He saw Mole coming down the road again. Bear was ready for him.

Bear took off one red paper shoe. He put it in the road. He wanted to get Mole's attention. Then Bear hid.

Along came Mole.

"What a nice shoe!" he said.

"Too bad there is just one."

He left the shoe in the road.

Then he walked on.

Bear took the shoe and ran ahead.
He put the same shoe in the road.
Then Bear hid. He wanted to get
Mole's attention again.

Along came Mole again. He saw the beautiful paper shoe in the road.

"Look! Here is the other shoe. If I go back for the other one, I will have two," Mole said.

He put down the large jug. Then he ran back to get the other shoe.

Bear drank some water from the jug. He closed his eyes. Then he drank some more.

Bear left a little water for Mole.
Mole would need it when he got back.
Mole would not be happy.

Bear put on his shoes. His two beautiful, red paper shoes! Then he walked home to his family. Bear felt calm and cool now.

Bear's family liked the beautiful red paper shoes. They liked the flowers too. But most of all, they liked the story of Mole. And they loved hearing about how Bear got his long, cool drink of water.